PRINCE OF PERSIA
THE LOST CROWN

Master every Time Rift, Conquer every
Challenge and Unravel Qaf's Mysteries: Your
100% Completion Guide to The Lost Crown
(Gamer's Guide)

Levi Mateo Alexander

1

CONTENTS

THE WARRIOR

INTRODUCTION

The wind howls across Mount Qaf, a desolate realm where time itself seems fractured. Jagged peaks pierce the bruised sky, casting long, skeletal shadows across the cursed landscape. Here, whispers of a forgotten civilization dance on the thermals, echoing tales of a once-mighty empire and a crown forged from the very fabric of time.

But the echoes are broken, shattered by a curse that has shrouded the mountain in an eternal twilight. The once-vibrant city of Qafqa lies in ruin, its silent towers clutching at the clouds like skeletal fingers. And somewhere within this labyrinthine tomb of stone, a lost prince sleeps, his destiny intertwined with the fate of the slumbering city and the crown that holds the key to their awakening.

His name is Sargon, a young warrior whose veins hum with the whispers of an ancient lineage. He is no ordinary prince; within him lies the dormant power to manipulate time itself, a legacy passed down through generations of chronomancers. But Sargon's memories are as fragmented as the mountain he now walks. He remembers whispers of a betrayal, a stolen crown, and a curse that plunged Qaf into eternal twilight. He remembers a responsibility, a duty to reclaim his birthright and break the chains that bind his people.

His journey will be fraught with peril. Monstrous creatures stalk the shadows, woven from the darkest corners of time itself. Forgotten guardians, loyal to the usurper who stole the crown, lurk in the decaying ruins. And time, itself a fickle mistress, will play its top-down cruel games, twisting and turning, testing Sargon's resolve at every turn.

But Sargon is not alone. A band of enigmatic companions, each with their secrets and motivations, will guide him through the treacherous paths of Mount Qaf. There's the stoic warrior, her eyes reflecting the wisdom of countless battles, and the wisecracking thief, whose nimble fingers dance between treasure and danger. Together, they form a tapestry of loyalty and courage, a flickering flame against the encroaching darkness.

This is not just a story of a lost crown or a fallen city. It is a journey into the heart of time itself, a dance with destiny where every step echoes across millennia. It is a testament to the enduring power of hope, a whispered promise that even in the darkest night, a single spark can ignite the flames of rebellion and rewrite the very fabric of time.

So, turn the page, traveler. Let the sands of time guide you to the shattered gates of Qafqa. For within its crumbling walls, a prince awaits, and with him, the chance to rewrite a broken melody and reclaim a lost crown.

Are you ready to defy fate?

SARGON THE CONQUEROR

PART 1: UNRAVEL THE TANGLED THREADS OF FATE

Dive into a Forgotten Realm

Prepare to ascend the treacherous slopes of Mount Qaf, a realm shrouded in the chilling whispers of a forgotten civilization. In this forgotten land, time itself seems to twist and fracture, echoing with the remnants of a glorious, yet tragically cursed, past. Your guide becomes your torch, illuminating the secrets that lie buried beneath centuries of dust and decay.

Delve into the Grimoire of Qaf:

Uncover the Whispers of the Fallen: Explore ancient murals and cryptic carvings, piecing together the fragmented history of the Qafian Empire. Was it consumed by greed, consumed by time, or something more sinister?

Unravel the Curse of the Sands: Unmask the source of Mount Qaf's time-warping affliction. Is it a malevolent entity, a broken artifact, or a cosmic anomaly? Each clue holds the key to breaking the curse and restoring balance to the realm.

Meet the Echoes of the Past: Encounter spectral guardians, ghostly whispers, and even echoes of long-dead heroes. Their fragmented memories offer glimpses into the empire's downfall and potential paths to redemption.

Dauntless Exploration and Discovery:

Uncharted Tombs and Crumbling Citadels: Navigate labyrinthine ruins, solve environmental puzzles, and uncover hidden chambers brimming with forgotten treasures and lore. Each step reveals another piece of the Qafian puzzle.

Time-Fractured Landscapes: Traverse through temporal rifts, warping between past, present, and distorted echoes of the future. Witness the empire's rise and fall firsthand, and uncover secrets hidden within the folds of time.

Whispering Sands and Forbidden Libraries: Decipher ancient scrolls and dusty tomes, deciphering cryptic prophecies and forgotten rituals. The sands themselves hold secrets, whispering tales of forgotten kings and lost magic.

Beyond the Lore: A Gripping Narrative:

Forge Alliances with the Lost: Aid the enigmatic Qafian survivors, each with their own motivations and secrets. Their stories intertwine with yours, shaping the fate of Mount Qaf and potentially your own.

Confront the Harbingers of Oblivion: Face corrupted guardians, time-warped monstrosities, and enigmatic figures who seek to exploit the rift in time for their own gain. Each encounter is a thrilling test of your combat prowess and strategic thinking.

Unravel Your Own Destiny: The fate of Mount Qaf rests on your shoulders. Will you break the curse and restore balance, or succumb to the siren song of power and become another echo in the realm's forgotten past?

This is not just a journey through a forgotten realm, it's a descent into the heart of mystery and intrigue. Prepare to be captivated by the chilling lore, the haunting landscapes, and the thrilling narrative that awaits you on Mount Qaf. The secrets of the lost civilization are yours to discover, but be warned, the threads of fate are tangled, and every choice you make could unravel the very fabric of time itself.

Are you ready to become the chronicler of Mount Qaf's forgotten story?

Reforge a Shattered Legacy

Mount Qaf whispers of a forgotten legacy, a crown imbued with ancestral power and a chilling curse. As the Prince, it's your destiny to reclaim this lost treasure, not just for its temporal mastery, but to untangle the web of fate that binds you and this cursed realm.

Embrace the Mantle of Destiny:

Whispers of the Past: Uncover the chilling history of Mount Qaf, its once-thriving civilization, and the cataclysmic event that plunged it into darkness. Delve into ancient texts, decipher forgotten symbols, and piece together the fragmented tapestry of the past.

The lineage of Time Masters: Discover the Prince's true heritage, his bloodline's connection to the lost crown, and its power to manipulate the very fabric of time itself. Embrace the legacy of your ancestors and master the sands that flow through your veins.

A Web of Intrigue: Navigate a treacherous landscape of alliances and betrayals. Forge uneasy partnerships with enigmatic allies, each harboring their own secrets and agendas. Trust no one, but learn to discern truth from deception in this game of shadows.

Reclaim the Lost Crown:

Shattered Fragments: The lost crown lies in pieces, scattered across the treacherous peaks and hidden within ancient ruins. Follow the whispers of the wind, solve environmental puzzles, and decipher cryptic clues to hunt down each fragment and reunite the symbol of your power.

Trials of Time: Each fragment of the crown is guarded by its own trial, a test of your skills and mastery over time. Master parkour acrobatics to scale dizzying heights, manipulate time to overcome seemingly impossible obstacles, and hone your combat prowess to vanquish time-warped guardians.

Beyond Mortality: As you reclaim each fragment, the crown's power grows, unlocking new abilities and bending time to your will. Rewind your mistakes, relive epic moments, and even create temporal clones to strategize and conquer seemingly impossible challenges.

Confront the Shadows of the Past:

The Usurper's Curse: The lost crown is not just a symbol of power, but a conduit for a malevolent entity that has plunged Mount Qaf into darkness. Unmask the true villain, a figure shrouded in mystery, whose motives intertwine with the Prince's ancestral bloodline.

Breaking the Chains of Time: The curse of Mount Qaf ripples through time itself, distorting the fabric of reality. Discover the source of the curse and utilize your time-warping abilities to break its hold, not only on the mountain but on your own destiny.

Reforging the Future: Reclaiming the crown and breaking the curse is not just a personal quest, but a chance to rewrite the history of Mount Qaf. Shape the future of this forgotten land, forge new alliances, and leave your mark on the sands of time.

This is your guide to finding the lost crown, and a journey to reclaim your legacy and rewrite the fate of a cursed realm.

Navigate a Web of Intrigue

In the windswept peaks of Mount Qaf, time's threads are frayed and whispers of a fallen civilization hang heavy in the air. As the Prince, you stand at the precipice of destiny, burdened with the weight of a shattered legacy and the echoes of a chilling curse. But you are not alone.

Embark on a treacherous odyssey to reclaim the lost crown, a symbol of ancestral power and the key to unlocking the secrets of time itself. Along the way, you'll navigate a web of intrigue, where enigmatic allies hold the pieces to unmasking the true villain and unraveling the curse. Brace yourself, Prince, for each ally harbors a hidden past, whispering truths tangled with deceit and shrouded in forgotten lore.

Meet Farah, the enigmatic warrior: Skilled in the ancient arts of combat and steeped in the secrets of Mount Qaf, she holds the key to understanding the cursed history of the land. But a shadow haunts her past, one that binds her to the fate of the lost crown and threatens to engulf you both in its darkness.

Befriend Kadir, the cunning trickster: With nimble fingers and a silver tongue, he can unlock hidden pathways and manipulate the very fabric of time. His knowledge of the labyrinthine tunnels beneath

Mount Qaf is invaluable, but trust comes at a price – Kadir's own motives remain shrouded in mystery.

Unravel the secrets of Tahmine, the mystical guardian: Her wisdom echoes through the ancient ruins, guiding you through the tangled threads of prophecy. But her allegiance is as cryptic as the prophecies themselves, leaving you to question whether she is friend or foe in this twisted game of fate.

Forge alliances of necessity, but tread carefully. Each ally is a double-edged sword, offering invaluable aid while hiding secrets that could unravel your quest. As you delve deeper into the mystery, the lines between friend and foe blur, forcing you to confront the chilling truth: not all who offer a helping hand are who they seem.

Prepare to unravel a conspiracy that spans centuries, where loyalty is a fleeting ember and betrayal lurks in every whispered word. Can you navigate the treacherous web of intrigue, forge alliances with a clear conscience, and reforge your shattered legacy? The fate of Mount Qaf, and your own destiny, hangs in the balance.

PART 2: CONQUER EVERY CHALLENGE WITH TIME AS YOUR WEAPON

Become a Parkour Prodigy

Ascend to legendary heights, defy gravity with acrobatic grace, and navigate treacherous landscapes with the confidence of a true Prince. This section unlocks your inner parkour master and equips you to conquer every platforming challenge in Prince of Persia: The Lost Crown.

I. Mastering the Art of Movement:

Anatomy of an Acrobatic Prince: Understand the Prince's full range of movement, from agile wall runs and gravity-defying leaps to wall jumps and daring dives. This guide dissects each move and reveals hidden techniques for maximum fluidity.

Conquering the Vertical World: Master the art of scaling towering ruins and crumbling structures. Learn optimal wall-run chains, strategic use of grapple points, and hidden pathways for a truly acrobatic ascent.

Horizontal Mastery: Unleash your inner parkour artist on expansive platforms and perilous walkways. Learn to chain together air dashes, wall grinds, and precision jumps to navigate intricate landscapes with unparalleled speed and style.

II. Secrets of the Sands:

Time Your Moves: Bend time itself to your advantage during platforming challenges. Rewind missed jumps, extend wall runs, and defy gravity with perfectly timed chronomancy. This guide reveals the secrets of manipulating time for ultimate platforming mastery.

Unleash the Echoes: Utilize the Prince's Echo abilities to create temporary platforms and extend your reach. Learn clever combinations and strategic placements to overcome seemingly impossible gaps and reach hidden areas.

Combat Flow: Don't let enemies disrupt your parkour rhythm! Integrate combat seamlessly into your movements, using disarms, dodges, and aerial attacks to maintain momentum and conquer platforming challenges while dispatching foes.

III. Beyond the Basics:

Hidden Pathways and Shortcuts: Discover secret routes, hidden ledges, and acrobatic shortcuts that bypass lengthy platforming sections. This guide becomes your map to uncovering the fastest and most stylish ways to navigate Mount Qaf.

Master Trials: Push your parkour skills to the limit with optional challenge chambers. Learn advanced techniques, unlock hidden rewards, and etch your name amongst the true parkour masters.

With this comprehensive guide, you'll become an unstoppable force of movement, weaving through intricate landscapes and defying gravity with newfound confidence. Remember, practice makes perfect – so hone your skills, embrace the flow of time, and prepare to conquer every platforming challenge in Prince of Persia: The Lost Crown!

Unleash the Sands of Time

Rewind, reset, reignite – in Prince of Persia: The Lost Crown, time is your ultimate weapon. This section of your guide will transform you from a fledgling sandpiper into a master chronomancer, bending the flow of time to your will and conquering every obstacle in your path.

I. Rewind, Reflect, Redefine:

Harness the Sands: Master the mechanics of rewinding. Learn to instantly undo missteps, evade enemy attacks, and even create strategic loops for platforming mastery.

Embrace the Echoes: Uncover the secrets of Time Echoes. Relive past moments to activate switches, solve puzzles, and even unlock hidden areas inaccessible in the present.

Perfect Your Precision: Hone your rewind timing to pull off daring stunts and stylish combat takedowns. Slow down time mid-air, redirect projectiles, and become a whirlwind of acrobatic prowess.

II. Unravel the Mysteries of Chronomancy:

Unlock the Time Rifts: Navigate the fractures in time itself. Uncover alternate realities, explore forgotten timelines, and discover secrets lost to the ages.

Befriend the Time Guardians: Master the art of Chronoshifting. Befriend these ethereal beings, manipulating their abilities to slow down time, freeze enemies, and even launch devastating temporal attacks.

Defy the Sands of Corruption: Face formidable adversaries wielding corrupted time magic. Learn to counter their abilities, exploit their weaknesses, and reclaim the Sands of Time for your own purposes.

III. Master the Art of Time Warfare:

Unleash the Chronoblades: Hone your swordsmanship with these time-altering blades. Freeze enemies mid-strike, unleash devastating combos that warp through time, and become a dance of temporal death.

Conquer Time Trials: Put your mastery to the test in hidden Time Trials. Speed through intricate challenges, rewind your mistakes with precision, and claim bragging rights as the ultimate master of time.

Become a Legend of Time Manipulation: Combine your rewind skills, combat prowess, and knowledge of Chronoshifting to create your own unique combat style. Share your strategies with the community and leave your mark on the world of The Lost Crown.

By delving into these depths of temporal power, you'll transform your Prince into a time-bending juggernaut, effortlessly conquering every challenge and etching your name in the annals of chronomancy legend. Make your guide the ultimate resource for aspiring masters of time in The Lost Crown!

Defy Formidable Foes

The sands of time shift, revealing a panorama of adversaries who stand between you and reclaiming the lost crown. From corrupted guardians twisted by the curse to time-warping monstrosities defying the laws of nature, each encounter demands tactical mastery and a deft hand with your chronomancy. This guide equips you with the knowledge to dissect their weaknesses and unleash devastating combat strategies, transforming you from a mere warrior into a master of time itself.

1. Corrupted Guardians:

These twisted remnants of Qaf's fallen civilization patrol the ruins, wielding warped versions of the Prince's own abilities.

Sand Warriors: Mimic the Prince's parkour skills, but their movements are predictable. Use Time Rewind to dodge their attacks and counter with devastating combos.

Shieldbearers: Their shields deflect your blades. Disarm them with Time Freeze or use the environment to launch them off platforms.

Chronomancers: These warped mages can slow time, creating a treacherous dance. Use Time Warp to counter their ability, then unleash a flurry of attacks before they recover.

2. Time-Warped Monstrosities:

Defying the laws of physics and logic, these creatures blur the line between past and present, presenting unique challenges.

Chrono Serpents: These serpentine entities rewind time on contact, undoing your progress. Use Time

Rewind to counter their rewind, trapping them in a temporal loop and leaving them vulnerable.

Time Rifts: These ethereal portals spawn illusions that attack you. Close the rifts with Time Freeze, then focus on the real enemy lurking in the shadows.

Sand Golems: These hulking constructs crumble into sand when hit, but reform in the blink of an eye. Use Time Warp to slow their reformation, then strike while their form is incomplete.

3. Master of Time Combat Strategies:

Beyond individual enemies, hone your skills with these advanced tactics:

Time Strike: Freeze an enemy mid-attack, then rewind time and unleash a devastating counter blow.

Chronoshadow: Use Time Warp to create a temporary doppelganger, confusing enemies and allowing you to flank or heal.

Sand Trap: Invert the flow of time, making enemies walk backward into environmental hazards you've already set.

4. Hidden Depths:

Each foe holds secrets waiting to be discovered.

Parry and Counters: Learn the timing and rhythm of each enemy's attacks to unleash perfect parries and devastating counters.

Environmental Mastery: Use the landscape to your advantage. Throw enemies into sand pits, hurl them off platforms, or trigger hidden traps to turn the tide of battle.

Hidden Weaknesses: Some enemies are vulnerable to specific amulets or upgrades. Experiment to discover their Achilles' heel.

Remember, the sands of time are your canvas. Paint a masterpiece of strategized combat, and claim your place as the ultimate master of time and prince of Persia!

MASTER OF TIME

PART 3: EMBRACE THE MYSTERIES HIDDEN WITHIN

Unlock the Secrets of Time Rifts

Mount Qaf whispers of forgotten secrets, its jagged peaks pierced by shimmering portals that promise glimpses into alternate realities. These Time Rifts, however, are more than mere curiosities; they hold the key to understanding the mountain's cursed past and, perhaps, the path to breaking its hold. This guide will be your torch as you delve into these temporal abysses, unearthing lost echoes and piecing together the fragmented history of this enigmatic realm.

1. Echoes of the Fallen:

Whispers of Antiquity: Each rift whispers of a different era, from the opulent courts of a lost civilization to the desolate ruins of a fallen empire. Explore these fragments of history, deciphering murals, deciphering cryptic texts, and encountering spectral echoes of the past. This guide will point you toward hidden clues and unveil the stories etched into every temporal shard.

Echo Quests: Certain rifts hold the memories of forgotten tasks, and unfinished quests left by the lost inhabitants of Mount Qaf. Embark on these echo quests, retracing their steps and resolving their ancient grievances. Not only will you uncover valuable resources and lore, but you might even alter the fabric of time itself, influencing the present in unforeseen ways.

2. Temporal Puzzles:

Chronological Conundrums: Time Rifts are not merely portals; they are intricate puzzles woven from the threads of history. Solve temporal enigmas by manipulating the flow of time within the rift, aligning objects, activating dormant mechanisms, and even altering the sequence of events to unlock the path forward. This guide will provide hints, strategies, and alternative solutions to every temporal conundrum, ensuring you never get lost in the labyrinth of time.

Temporal Echoes: These enigmatic wisps of energy hold fragments of knowledge and forgotten skills. Collect them within the rifts and watch as they resonate with your own chronomancy, unlocking new abilities and augmenting your mastery over time itself. This guide will map the locations of these echoes, allowing you to maximize your temporal arsenal and become a true master of the Sands.

3. Guardians of the Past:

Wraiths of Time: Not all who dwell within the Time Rifts are welcoming spirits. Corrupted guardians, warped by the fractured flow of time, stand between you and the secrets you seek. Master the art of combat within these chaotic landscapes, adapting your strategies to each temporal anomaly and exploiting the weaknesses of these twisted foes. This guide will offer detailed combat strategies and insights into the nature of these temporal guardians, ensuring you emerge victorious from every temporal battle.

The Time Weaver: Deep within the labyrinth of rifts lies a being of immense power, the Time Weaver. This entity controls the very fabric of time within Mount Qaf, and its motives are shrouded in mystery. Confront this enigmatic being, unraveling its secrets and facing the ultimate challenge of your time-warping journey. This guide will prepare you for this epic showdown, offering insights into Time Weaver's abilities and strategies to overcome its temporal dominion.

Remember, the Time Rifts are not mere distractions; they are the beating heart of Mount Qaf's secrets. Embrace the mysteries they hold, navigate their labyrinthine depths, and emerge with the knowledge to reshape the present and rewrite the past itself. This guide will be your constant companion, your compass in the tangled tapestry of time.

Haunt for lost treasures

Prepare to embark on a perilous treasure hunt, fellow Prince! Within the crumbling ruins and sun-scorched sands of Mount Qaf lie secrets waiting to be unearthed. This guide will be your compass as you navigate a labyrinth of hidden chambers, forgotten pathways, and cryptic clues, leading you to a trove of invaluable riches and untold glory.

Unmask the Jewels of Power:

Amulets of Antiquity: Scour every nook and cranny for potent amulets imbued with ancient magic. This guide reveals their hidden locations, unlocking abilities like time-warping shields, devastating elemental attacks, and the power to teleport through walls.

Relics of a Lost Civilization: Unearth fragments of a shattered past, piecing together the history of Mount Qaf's fallen inhabitants. Each relic unlocks bonus content, including concept art, lore entries, and exclusive challenges.

Bonus Content Bonanza: From hidden parkour courses to time trial arenas, this guide exposes every secret level and bonus objective. Maximize your playtime and claim bragging rights as a true master of The Lost Crown.

Become a Master Treasure Hunter:

Deciphering the Dunes: Learn to interpret the whispers of the desert wind and cryptic environmental clues. This guide teaches you to recognize hidden markings, activate pressure plates, and unlock secret doors veiled by illusion.

Puzzles of Plutus: Sharpen your mind with intricate environmental puzzles guarding the most valuable treasures. This guide provides step-by-step solutions and insightful hints to conquer every riddle, from logic puzzles to timed trials.

Echoes of the Past: Follow the whispers of time rifts and uncover hidden chambers holding relics and echoes of the past. This guide reveals the activation triggers and hidden pathways, allowing you to delve into forgotten memories and uncover the truth about Mount Qaf's demise.

Leave No Stone Unturned:

Interactive Treasure Map: A detailed, interactive map pinpoints every hidden treasure, amulet, and bonus content location. Track your progress, share your discoveries with fellow adventurers, and never miss a single secret.

Completionist Checklist: Stay on track with a comprehensive checklist detailing every collectible, bonus objective, and secret area. Achieve 100% completion and bask in the satisfaction of conquering every challenge The Lost Crown offers.

The Ultimate Trophy Guide: Unlock every achievement and platinum trophy with precision-crafted strategies and tips. This guide reveals all the hidden requirements and Easter eggs, ensuring you leave no achievement ungripped.

Remember, the thrill of the hunt is half the reward! Follow this guide, hone your detective skills, and prepare to be dazzled by the hidden wonders of Mount Qaf. Claim every amulet, unearth every relic, and unlock every bonus secret. With this guide as your torch, 100% completion and legendary status are within your grasp!

Crack the cryptic puzzle

The Sands of Time whisper secrets, ancient relics gleam with forgotten power, and hidden amulets promise to rewrite your destiny. In this chapter, you'll become a master treasure hunter, unlocking every bonus and leaving no secret unturned.

I. Unearthing the Unseen:

The Treasure Hunter's Handbook: Master the art of deciphering cryptic symbols, following hidden pathways, and activating secret switches. This guide becomes your decoder ring, revealing the language of lost civilizations.

Map Mania: Dive into detailed maps of each realm, revealing every hidden nook, treacherous cranny, and suspicious crack in the wall. Let no treasure remain unclaimed!

Whispers in the Wind: Listen closely to the whispers of the Sands. They'll guide you toward hidden caches, activate secret doors, and reveal the locations of long-lost relics.

II. A Collector's Paradise:

Amulets of Power: Unearth every hidden amulet, unlocking unique abilities that enhance your combat, parkour, and time-manipulation skills. This guide will lead you to each one, maximizing your potential as the Prince.

Relics of Renown: Discover ancient relics scattered across Mount Qaf, each holding a piece of the forgotten lore. These treasures not only enrich your understanding of the world but also unlock bonus content and special rewards.

Hidden Chambers of Riches: From glittering gold chests to secret merchant stashes, track down every hidden treasure trove and amass a fortune fit for a king. This guide will be your key to unlocking untold wealth.

III. Beyond the Obvious:

Environmental Secrets: Look beyond the surface! Walls may shift, floors may crumble, and seemingly innocuous objects might hold hidden triggers. This guide unveils the environmental puzzles waiting to be solved, granting access to hidden areas and bonus content.

Time Rifts and Twisted Paths: Traverse alternate realities within time rifts to reach hidden chambers, uncover forgotten stories, and collect unique treasures. This guide will be your compass through the labyrinthine tapestry of time.

Completionist's Compendium: Track every collectible, every bonus objective, and every hidden achievement with our comprehensive checklist. This guide will be your oath of completion, ensuring you leave no corner of Mount Qaf unexplored.

Remember, the greatest treasure lies not in gold or jewels, but in the thrill of the hunt and the satisfaction of piecing together the mysteries of The Lost Crown. This guide will be your faithful companion, leading you to every hidden secret and ensuring you become the ultimate explorer of Mount Qaf.

PART 4: MASTER THE ART OF BEING A PRINCE

Forge Your Legend in The Lost Crown

Embrace your inner warrior, hone your skills, and become the Prince of Persia you were always meant to be! This section is your ultimate guide to optimizing your playstyle, crafting a legend, and conquering The Lost Crown with unparalleled finesse.

I. Amulets: Your Arsenal of Time-Bending Power:

The Sands of Chronos: Rewind time itself, evade attacks, and set up devastating combos. Master this amulet to become a temporal phantom, leaving enemies bewildered and defeated.

The Eye of Eternity: Slow down time, unleash devastating charged attacks, and conquer platforming challenges with pinpoint precision. This amulet transforms you into a master of control, dictating the flow of battle and defying gravity.

The Fury of the Djinn: Unchain your inner beast with this amulet's rage-fueled attacks. Unleash a whirlwind of blades, shatter defenses, and dominate head-on brawls. This is the path for those who revel in the roar of battle.

The Veil of Shadows: Become a silent predator with this amulet's cloak of invisibility. Slip past enemies undetected, execute stealthy takedowns, and manipulate the environment for tactical advantage. This is the way of the cunning assassin, striking from the shadows with deadly precision.

II. Upgrades: Sharpen Your Skills and Unleash Your Potential:

Combat Mastery: Enhance your swordsmanship with faster attacks, parries, and devastating combos. Become a whirlwind of steel, leaving no enemy standing.

Parkour Prodigy: Hone your acrobatic skills with improved agility, wall-runs, and aerial maneuvers. Defy gravity, traverse treacherous landscapes, and outmaneuver your foes with breathtaking fluidity.

Chronomancer's Wisdom: Deepen your understanding of time manipulation. Extend time slows, unlock hidden chronomancy abilities, and bend the very fabric of time to your will.

Shadow's Embrace: Become a master of stealth with improved invisibility duration, silent takedowns, and environmental manipulation. Strike from the darkness, leaving your enemies whispering tales of the unseen terror.

III. Forge Your Legend: Crafting Your Unique Playstyle:

The Balanced Prince: Combine elements of combat mastery, parkour prowess, and chronomancy to become a versatile warrior, adapting to any situation with grace and skill.

The Time-Warping Assassin: Embrace the Eye of Eternity and Shadow's Embrace. Slow down time, strike from the shadows, and manipulate the environment to become a silent, deadly reaper.

The Unstoppable Berserker: Unleash the Fury of the Djinn and Combat Mastery. Charge into battle, unleash devastating combos, and break through any defense with brute force.

The Ghostly Acrobat: Master the Veil of Shadows and Parkour Prodigy. Move unseen, scale impossible heights, and execute acrobatic takedowns, becoming a phantom that strikes without warning.

Remember, there is no single "best" path. Experiment, discover what suits your playstyle, and forge your own legend in the sands of time.

Bonus Tips:

- Synergy is key: Combine amulets and upgrades to unlock powerful combos and hidden abilities.
- Adapt to the challenge: Each enemy and environment requires a different approach. Use your skills and knowledge to overcome any obstacle.
- Master the challenges: Seek out hidden trials and arenas to test your skills and unlock exclusive rewards.

With this guide as your compass, you are ready to conquer The Lost Crown and etch your name in the annals of Prince of Persia lore. Go forth, champion! The sands of time await your mastery!

Conquer the Unthinkable

Beyond the standard challenges, The Lost Crown holds hidden realms of difficulty waiting to test the mettle of even the most seasoned Prince. This section will equip you with the knowledge and strategies to conquer these ultimate trials, emerging not just victorious, but as the embodiment of true princely prowess.

Hidden Boss Battles:

The Time Weaver: This enigmatic being manipulates time itself, creating illusions and shifting platforms. Use your chronomancy to counter their attacks, rewind to dodge time-warping projectiles, and strike when their defenses are weakest.

The Sandsong Serpent: This colossal beast writhes through the sands, summoning sandstorms and unleashing devastating sonic attacks. Time your dodges to avoid its crushing coils, manipulate the environment to create temporary platforms, and unleash a focused Sands of Time attack to pierce its armored hide.

The Lost King: A corrupted echo of the Prince's ancestors, wielding a corrupted version of the lost crown. Master your combat skills to counter his mirror image attacks, utilize time manipulation to disrupt his chronomancy, and ultimately reclaim the crown's true power.

Secret Trials:

The Sands of Regret: This gauntlet tests your platforming prowess and time-bending mastery. Navigate intricate sand-shifting platforms, rewind mistakes to avoid crumbling pathways, and utilize time manipulation to create shortcuts and unlock hidden secrets.

The Echoes of Time: This trial challenges your combat skills and strategic thinking. Face waves of increasingly difficult enemies, utilize time manipulation to create tactical advantages and optimize your amulets and upgrades to overcome each wave.

The Prince's Paradox: This ultimate test pits you against a mirror image of yourself, perfectly replicating your moves and abilities. Master advanced combat techniques, learn to predict your opponent's moves, and utilize time manipulation to gain the upper hand and claim victory over your own shadow.

Tips for Princely Prowess:

Master the Art of Time Manipulation: Learn to rewind mistakes, slow down time for precise platforming, and unleash devastating time-warping attacks. Experiment with different combinations to find your perfect chronomancy style.

Unleash the Power of Your Amulets: Each amulet offers unique abilities and boons. Tailor your loadout to suit your playstyle, whether you prefer swift acrobatics, devastating combos, or tactical control of the battlefield.

Sharpen Your Combat Skills: Mastering perfect dodges, parries, and counters is crucial for conquering hidden bosses and trials. Practice different combat techniques, experiment with different weapons, and hone your reflexes to become a true master of swordsmanship.

Embrace the Parkour Master: The Prince's agility is his greatest asset. Learn advanced parkour moves, utilize the environment to your advantage, and discover hidden pathways to reach secret areas and uncover hidden treasures.

Seek the Wisdom of the Ancients: Explore hidden scrolls and murals to unlock ancient techniques and forgotten lore. These secrets can provide invaluable insights into the game's mechanics, hidden areas, and even boss strategies.

Remember, Prince:
- Patience is key. Don't rush through challenges, take your time to understand enemy patterns and strategize your approach.
- Experimentation is your friend. Try different combinations of amulets, weapons, and time manipulation to discover your most effective playstyle.
- Learn from your mistakes. Rewind when necessary, analyze what went wrong, and refine your approach to overcome any obstacle.
- Embrace the challenge. The toughest trials offer the greatest rewards. Rise to the occasion and claim your place as the ultimate Prince of Persia!

By mastering these strategies and embracing the challenges that await, you will rise above a mere prince and become the ultimate king of time and sand. Go forth, conquer the unthinkable, and etch your name in the legend of Prince of Persia!

Sharpen Your Skills

Embrace your destiny as the Prince of Persia with this ultimate guide to honing your skills and becoming a master of acrobatics, combat, and chronomancy. Leave your enemies breathless and challenges conquered with these exclusive training grounds, advanced techniques, and parkour mastery challenges!

I. The Prince's Playground: Your Training Grounds Await:

Parkour Prodigy Arena: Scale treacherous ruins, swing across perilous chasms, and defy gravity with precision in this dedicated parkour training ground. Master wall runs, chain slides, and aerial attacks, building your agility and confidence to navigate any platforming nightmare.

Combat Crucible: Hone your blade in this interactive combat arena. Face virtual foes programmed with diverse attack patterns and learn to counter, parry, and unleash devastating combos. Experiment with different combat styles, mastering swordsmanship, dagger finesse, and shield-bashing dominance.

Time Trial Chamber: Bend time to your will within the Time Trial Chamber. Replay challenging sections under the pressure of the clock, perfecting your speed, precision, and time manipulation skills to shave seconds off your runs and conquer speedrun glory.

II. Unlocking Combat Secrets: Techniques for a Prince's Arsenal:

Chronomancer Combo Mastery: Discover hidden synergies between your time powers and combat moves. Weave rewind strikes into devastating flurries, extend slow-motion dodges into lethal counters, and unleash time stasis-fueled aerial assaults that leave enemies flailing in mid-air.

Environmental Alchemy: Turn the environment into your weapon. Master the art of using terrain hazards, explosive barrels, and collapsible platforms to create chain reactions and obliterate enemies in creative, stylish ways.

Adaptive Strategies: Learn to read your foes. Identify enemy weaknesses, exploit elemental vulnerabilities, and switch between ranged and melee tactics on the fly to become an unstoppable force of adaptability.

III. Parkour Perfection: Defying Gravity, One Move at a Time:

Hidden Paths Revealed: Uncover secret routes and shortcuts on every map. This guide dissects every level, unveiling hidden ledges, grapple points, and wall-walking opportunities that bypass grueling challenges and grant you an edge over even the most seasoned explorers.

Mastering Movement Fluidity: Learn to chain together advanced parkour moves for unparalleled grace and efficiency. Discover hidden combos of wall runs, jumps, and dashes, transforming your traversal into a mesmerizing dance of defiance against gravity.

Environmental Creativity: Think outside the wall! This guide unlocks the potential of seemingly mundane objects. Learn to use ropes, cloth hangings, and even crumbling structures as improvised platforms and springboards, defying boundaries and opening up unexpected paths.

IV. Beyond the Basics: Pushing Your Princely Limits:

Boss Masterclass: Each colossal guardian requires a unique approach. This guide lays bare their attack patterns, weak points, and environmental triggers, allowing you to orchestrate their downfall with surgical precision and dazzling chronomancy.

100% Completion Challenge: Unlock every secret, collect every treasure, and unravel every mystery. This guide becomes your roadmap to 100% completion, guiding you to hidden collectibles, Easter eggs, and even alternate endings that reward meticulous exploration.

Speedrun Strategies: Shave minutes off your playtime and become a legend among players. This guide details optimal routes, time-saving glitches (if ethical), and advanced chronomancy tactics to propel you to leaderboard dominance.

Become the Prince you were born to be. With this guide, you'll possess the skills to navigate any treacherous landscape, disarm any enemy, and bend time itself to your will. Remember, Prince, the fate of Mount Qaf rests on your shoulders. Rise to the challenge, hone your skills, and reclaim your crown as the true master of The Lost Crown!

CONCLUSION

As the sands of time settle upon Mount Qaf, a new dawn breaks over the once-cursed realm. The Lost Crown sits upon its rightful brow, casting a radiant light that banishes the shadows of the past. Sargon stands tall, no longer a prince lost in the echoes of memory, but a king reborn, his lineage reclaimed, his destiny fulfilled.

His journey has transformed him. The trials he faced, the alliances he forged, and the sacrifices he made have etched themselves upon his soul. He has mastered the dance of time, learned to wield its power with wisdom and humility, and understood that even the mightiest chronomancer cannot control destiny alone.

Qafqa awakens from its slumber, its towers stretching towards the heavens as life pulses anew through its veins. The people, long burdened by the curse, emerge from their stone prisons, their eyes alight with hope and gratitude. They hail Sargon as their savior, their king, the one who restored their stolen light.

But victory does not come without its scars. Sargon bears the weight of those lost in the struggle, their names etched upon his heart. He knows that true peace is not merely the absence of conflict, but the enduring legacy of those who fought for it. And so, he vows to honor their sacrifice, to rebuild Qafqa into a beacon of unity and resilience, where time is not a tyrant, but a tapestry woven from shared memories and dreams.

The echoes of the past still linger, whispering tales of betrayal and resilience. But they are not a burden; they are a testament to the enduring strength of the human spirit. Sargon knows that the sands of time will continue to shift, that new challenges will arise, and that the dance with destiny is never truly over.

But he stands ready, his heart aflame with a newfound purpose. For he is no longer merely a prince, nor simply a king. He is the guardian of time, the weaver of destinies, and the keeper of the Lost Crown. And as long as he draws breath, he will protect his people, his legacy, and the very fabric of time itself.

So let the sands whisper his name, let the winds carry his tale, and let the echoes of his journey inspire those who seek to defy fate and reclaim their own lost crowns.

For the journey is not over. It has only just begun.

This book has been designed using assets from Istock.com, pexels.com and gettyimage.com